Superwoman Does Not Exist

Superwoman Does Not Exist

Kippie Martin

Kippie Publishing

Copyright © 2000 Kippie Martin
All rights reserved; no part of this publication may be reproduced, stored in a retrieval system, or transmitted, in any form or by any means, electronic, mechanical, photocopying, recording, or otherwise, without the prior written permission of the publisher.

Manufactured in the United States of America
Library of Congress Control Number: 00-091828
ISBN: 0-9679290-1-6
Cover art: Robert Giumarra
Book design and production: Tabby House
Cover design: OspreyDesign

Kippie Publishing
P.O. Box 225
Madison, CT 06443
(203) 318-8335
http://www.superwomandoesnotexist.com

Special thanks to God, who has allowed me to complete every project that I have started, and to the many family and friends who have supported me and helped out with my children as if they were their own. I love you all.

Kippie

Superwoman Does Not Exist!

The reason I have a hard time staying home and taking care of the family and house on a full-time basis is that I invested so many years in college pursuing another career.

Superwoman is a myth. Her real name is stressed-out woman.

You ask what I do all day? You wear them (the clothes I clean), you eat it (the food I cook) and you kiss them (your children).

Sometimes I get so stressed out that I want to go into a closet and cry, but I don't, because I know my kids will find me.

My profession is that of juggler because I eat, wash dishes, cook and clean—all at the same time!

Mothers can't afford to get sick—there's nobody to take care of us or our responsibilities.

I am fighting for my freedom or rebirth.

> Do you ever feel that you need a massive makeover when you go out to dinner?

Oh, joy! All this and menopause, too.

I thought I could give up coffee, but then I had another baby.

Yes, once upon a time, there was a woman who thought she could do it all, only to discover she couldn't.

I am part of the *new* women's movement. I am not trying to impress anyone by stressing myself out working inside and outside the home.

Moms and friends will tell new mothers to sleep while their baby sleeps, but what they fail to mention is that the dishes won't get washed, showers won't be taken, dinner won't get fixed and bottles won't be made. Baby naptime is mother worktime.

It's a bad thing to laugh too much if you're more than seven months pregnant.

If women knew what they were in for before they got married they wouldn't be so eager to run down the aisle.

I've begun to see how we let ourselves go. It's because we make everything and everyone more important than ourselves.

Mirror, mirror, on the wall, I can't believe what happened to me.

Today is just one of those give-up days.

My girlfriend apologized for not calling me for my birthday, but I told her there was no need to apologize because I understood how having a baby-sitter quit could affect a mother's mental state.

I realized that going to the best graduate school could not help me with parenting and marital skills. I had to call up the School of Reality where grandmothers are presidents, moms are vice presidents and fathers are consultants on providing strategies for their daughters.

Why is it that women, not men, must be the guinea pigs for every form of birth control?

I looked at the security guard while being wheeled out of the hospital with my newborn and said, "This is the last one!" He said, "That's what they all say!"

After becoming a mother, my small pocketbook has turned into a knapsack.

Do you ever get to a point in your life when you just don't care if every hair is in place or that you aren't as color coordinated as you used to be?

Laundromats are great because more than one load of clothes can be washed and dried at the same time.

I never thought I would see the day when I would stand straight, look down and not be able to see my feet—and it wasn't because my breasts were too large or because I was pregnant.

And if they think playing the stock market is a difficult job—they should try being a parent for a day.

I guess we women try to use every minute in a day to accomplish a million tasks because we feel it will free up time for us tomorrow, but it never seems to work that way because we always find other things to do.

I stopped sending my résumé to the human resource department because they don't understand how valuable and diversified my skills are from the years I have spent at home with my children. Instead, I send it to the CEO.

Time to ourselves? Is there such a thing?

I told my husband that if he continues to bring guests home without informing me in advance, what they see might amaze them.

> If it's not on the refrigerator, don't expect me to remember it.

Before marriage quote without kids: I want it all, husband, children and a six-figure job.

After marriage quote with kids: "You can't have the husband, children and a six-figure job and if you do, who's raising your children and sleeping with your husband?"

All I want for my birthday is for you to watch the kids for a day, cook, clean and don't ask me to do anything at all.

> I feel like an undervalued stock.

What upsets me most is when corporate America can't seem to find value in moms who have stayed home for years raising their children and later have decided to return to work outside the home

When I look at my kids and observe some of the things they do, I ask myself if I put my parents through the same things.

There's no such thing as feeling fine six weeks after giving birth.

A solution to the shortage of skilled workers would be to have daycare centers, doctors and fitness centers on the work premises.

Let it be known that I try to be a good mom and wife and if my best is not good enough, then it's just too bad.

The reason my hair is always in a ponytail and I wear shorts and a T-shirt is because the forty-five minutes I have to myself sometime during the week is used to work out on the treadmill. The only problem is that I never know when I'll have this time, so I have to be prepared or lose out on the opportunity.

I keep telling my husband that I'm the Playwoman—I'm not trying to do it all. The woman he thinks I should be can be found on television—the woman who handles working inside and outside the home, and wears a size-five dress above the knee. Her house is spotless, dinner is always prepared on time and the family is always cheery and presentable. I call her the Soap Opera Woman.

Isn't it funny how men don't see some things as a necessity until they are wearing our shoes?

It's not that I can't find anything *better* to do with my time, it's just the *only* thing I can do with my time.

Instead of a night out with the girls, I would rather a couple of hours of undisturbed sleep.

Moms are like glue. No matter how sticky the situation is, we keep it all together.

Beepers are for people who want to be on call twenty-four hours a day. I do believe that I am entitled to sleep.

I knew he was trying to make me feel good by saying I looked good, but how could I look good with brown shoes, white sweat socks, gray pants, a burgundy sweatshirt and every hair out of place?

The cashier apologized for taking so long, but I told her not to worry because my husband had all three toddlers at home with him.

My husband knows more about television shows than I do and I'm home all day.

When another woman told me that continuously buying paper plates could be costly, I told her eating out was even more.

When I told my cousin that I would be washing dishes, folding clothes and cooking dinner on my birthday, she told me that things had really changed in our lives.

I understand my eight-year-old had good intentions by wanting to celebrate my fortieth birthday, but making a card in school and having his whole class sign it, including his teacher, was a bit much.

I wonder if these people who write books on children have ever had kids themselves?

I told my girlfriend that only one of us can be in a mental institution at a time. The other one has to counsel.

After four births, I can't hold it anymore. When I have to go to the bathroom I better find one quickly.

Don't you find yourself saying, I just have to do this for me, regardless of whether anyone understands?

Help! Help! Let me out of here!
I am tired of being a prisoner in
solitary confinement.

Don't be fooled by appearances—everyone after a certain age gets wrinkles and gray hair.

The biggest joke I had was when I thought I would never ask for any painkillers while delivering my first baby. But by the time the first labor pain hit, I was screaming A-N-E-S-T-H-E-S-I-O-L-O-G-I-S-T!

I have transformed into someone who doesn't have to get her clothes dry-cleaned and her hair done every week. It has made my life a lot less stressful.

Beware, moms, if you want to get a job outside the home—overtime is generally required.

Procedures for going to the bathroom while holding your three-month-old. Using one hand, lock the bathroom door, get the toilet paper, pull up/down your clothes, use the toilet paper, pull up your clothes, flush the toilet with your foot, open the door and wash your hands.

The only time we get the care we need is when we're in the hospital having a baby. I guess the nurses know what we're in for when we get home.

Annoyed, I felt I really had to take a stand after the interviewer told me that although I presented a solid case for someone who could do the job, I didn't have the right certifications. I told him I had the certification of motherhood and there was no certification out there that could top that.

My husband thinks he's the one who
can't wait until he retires so
that he can be home with the kids.
He's mistaken—I can't wait.

My kids feel that it's all right to have a conversation with me while I'm on the toilet. I've resorted to locking the door.

The only time I came close to having a superwoman episode was when I was in the hospital having contractions the day before I was to graduate from graduate school. The contractions stopped the next morning and I had enough time to shower, go home and change my clothes and attend my afternoon graduation. I had the baby three days later.

It's funny that men come home from work, tell you how hard they worked all day and ask you to bring them their dinner.

I thought being successful was rising quickly up the corporate ladder, but now I realize it means being able to stay married for twenty years, raising great kids and putting God first!

Why is it that we're never recognized for the 100 things we do right, only criticized for the one thing we didn't do?

Whenever I go out for a romantic evening, my neighbor laughs as I walk out the door with my fancy dress on, high heels, a baby bag in one hand and the baby in the other. Oops! I had to run back in for the bottles.

Never wear a girdle to hide those slight imperfections because you will begin to believe that it will work for the rest of your life.

VCRs, dishwashers, microwaves and computers haven't freed up more of my time, they have just made me try to do more things at once.

> I can only accomplish what time
> and peace of mind allows me to do.

Until now I didn't understand why there is so much fuss made over brides on their wedding day. It is because it is the only day they get the respect and attention they deserve.

I don't know if my husband really doesn't see the clothes on the floor as he leaps over them or if he's just practicing for some worldwide competition.

I should have obeyed my aunt when she tried to restrain me from catching the bride's bouquet at my cousin's wedding. I know now that she was trying to tell me something.

When my husband came home and looked at our messy home with a disgusted look on his face, I smiled sweetly, and told him there's always tomorrow.

The perfect cooking show would be one that didn't require a whole lot of spices or measuring and would show me how to make a variety of meals using the same basic ingredients with a little modification. My kids are getting tired of plain white rice and mashed potatoes.

Although I now work nine to five outside the house, Monday through Friday, it's only considered my part-time job. The real full-time job starts between the hours of 5:01 P.M. and 8:59 A.M.

My most embarrassing moment was when I came out of a concert in New York City and realized that the top part of my shirt was soaked because I didn't use my breast pads.

> Why is it that we only seem to get recognized for the work we do outside the house?

We seem to be in the business of pampering everyone else but ourselves.

> Why are we expected to
> know it all,
> do it all,
> be it all?

Eliminate wasted time, it's a waste of your time.

The best advice I can give to other women like me is, don't waste your time on the success of others. Invest in your own success, because you are worth it!

For additional copies of this book send check or money order in the amount of $8.95 for each copy, plus $4 shipping and handling (add $1 additional S&H for each additional copy) to:

Superwoman Does Not Exist

P.O. Box 225,

Madison, CT 06443

Connecticut residents must add 6% sales tax

Sorry, no credit cards

<u>Ship to:</u>

Name:

Address:

City, State, Zip

To be put on the mailing list for the second volume send your name and address to above address.

About the author

Kippie Martin has an undergraduate degree from Bernard Baruch College and a master of arts degree from Teachers College, Columbia University, specializing in communication, computing and technology in education. She is an assistive technology specialist for individuals with special needs.

She began jotting down her thoughts about motherhood, being a wife, and staying home after her fourth child was born. Sleepless nights, endless diaper changes, breastfeeding, moving, job hunting as her husband was transferred out of state and Kippie asked, "OK, Lord, what's next?" The answer was this book.